Jealous Lion

FINDS FRIENDS

Pattie Thomas & Julian Nunnally

Art by Pattie Thomas

2013 Pattie Thomas and Julian Nunnally, ALL RIGHTS RESERVED.

No part of this book may be reproduced, stored in a retrieval system or transmitted by any means--recording, mechanical, electronic, photocopy, or otherwise without the written permission of the authors.

ISBN-10: 061598226
ISBN-13: 97801928227

Published by JellybeanPress 12/12/2012

Bring authors to your live event. For more information or to book an event contact www.pattiethomas.com (Speakers Bureau).

Proceeds from Jealous Lion are donated to visually impaired charities.

Dedication

I dedicate this book to GOD who is the light of my life. He has blessed me with so many gifts and talents to share with others. Kee' Lani (my granddaughter) has inspired me to keep my faith; Toni Smiley kept me focused to believe; Darcell Ezell made me laugh and keep pushing my writing and drawing. Talia Robinson just arrived in this world to love and my nephew Donte who loves his Auntie. Also, to all my readers and their families who believe in greatness.

I THANK YOU.
Pattie Thomas

This book gives GOD glory and being grateful. I love you Mom!
Julian Nunnally

Introduction

Jealous lion has no friends because of a selfish attitude until hunters try and capture him. He makes the correct choice to be friends with other jungle animals.

They teach Jealous Lion to always keep a good attitude in life. Jealous Lion teaches children life skills in a fun way.

Once upon a time in a far away jungle, there lived a lion that was jealous of everything and everybody.

Lion was jealous because the other animals didn't want to be his friend due to his bad attitude.

On the other side of the jungle there was Tiger, who was very nice and didn't like any fighting.

He enjoyed having parties, which were held every Friday at 5 o'clock.

Lion said, " Get away from me before I yell at you too!" Tiger laughed and Lion said, "You won't obey me?" When Tiger stopped laughing, he saw Lion's mouth with sharp teeth showing. Lion yelled at Tiger.

Tiger shook his head and said, "He needs a friend."

The next day was Tiger's party in which all the jungle animals were there except for the Jealous Lion.

The food was great! At the party there were peanuts for the elephants, fruit for the monkeys and gorillas, and worms for the birds.

Tiger was happy to show his friends hospitality.

As the animals danced, they heard Lion roaring ferociously in a tree. Hunters were in the jungle and tried to capture him.

The animals left the party and ran to help Lion including Tiger.
When the animals found Lion, he was in a net.

Lion said, "Thank you for saving me!" Tiger said, "No problem. Do you want to come to my party?" "Sure," said Lion. Lion changed his attitude and finally stopped being jealous. Then he became the king of the jungle.

~ *Moral* ~

The moral of the story is that it is better to be nice than to be mean and friends will help you.

THE END

Bring Pattie to Your School

Pattie is passionate about reading, creating, and writing. She shares this passion in lively, interactive presentations. Equally comfortable with large groups or small, she speaks to many children during a visit.

Pattie tailors each presentation to suit the children, in this way providing them the best experience possible. Children are engaged in dialogue and discussions focusing on life skills and behavior in a fun way.

Pattie has been a featured speaker at conferences, workshops, panels, and as a critic.

To schedule a booking visit:
www.pattiethomas.com

About the Authors

Pattie Thomas has worked in entertainment for 17+ years, teaching, creating, and servings arts & culture for all age groups. She loves to write and help others through written words and images. Pattie lives in Chicago. She has two children, a granddaughter, and her turtle Godzilla has not learned to read yet. So she listens to Pattie's stories.

More titles by Pattie Thomas "Other People Issues"
Visit www.pattiethomas.com

Julian Nunnally learned to write stories with his mom in elementary school and won young author awards. He resides in Chicago and holds a bachelor's degree in Exercise Science.

JellybeanPress

www.ingramcontent.com/pod-product-compliance
Lightning Source LLC
Chambersburg PA
CBHW041946110426
42744CB00027B/27